MAKE YOUR OWN CHEESE

SELF-SUFFICIENT RECIPES FOR CHEDDAR, PARMESAN, ROMANO, CREAM CHEESE, MOZZARELLA, COTTAGE CHEESE & FETA

D1609885

Caleb Warnock

THE BACKYARD RENAISSANCE COLLECTION

DISCOVER THE
LONG-LOST SKILLS OF
SELF-RELIANCE

My name is Caleb Warnock, and I've been working for years to learn how to return to forgotten skills, the skills of our ancestors. As our world becomes increasingly unstable, self-reliance becomes invaluable. Throughout this series, *Backyard Renaissance*, I will share with you the lost skills of self-sufficiency and healthy living. Come with me and other do-it-yourself experimenters, and rediscover the joys and success of simple self-reliance.

FAMILIUS

Copyright © 2015 by Caleb Warnock

Published by Familius LLC, www.familius.com

Familius books are available at special discounts for bulk purchases for sales
promotions or for family or corporate use. Special editions, including personalized
covers, excerpts of existing books, or books with corporate logos, can be created in
large quantities for special needs. For more information, contact Premium Sales at
559-876-2170 or email specialmarkets@familius.com.

pISBN 978-1-939629-74-6
eISBN 978-1-942672-07-4

Cover and book design by David Miles
Edited by Lindsay Sandberg

10 9 8 7 6 5 4 3 2 1

First Edition

CONTENTS

Cheese has been a sore spot for me for a long time. If you have read any of my books, you know that I am big on self-reliance. I knew people had self-sufficiently made cheese for thousands of years, but I had not been able to find anyone who knew how to make self-reliant *hard* cheese. Now I want to share my cheesy success with you.

8 PERFECT REASONS

to Make Caleb Warnock's

SELF-RELIANT

HOMEMADE CHEESE:

1. My recipe, which I worked for hundreds of hours to create, is available nowhere else. You won't find a do-it-yourself cheese-making method anywhere on the Internet!

2. It's simple. Once you have practiced the recipe a couple of times, "the cheese practically makes itself," as a friend of mine says.

3. My recipes cost 30 percent less than store-bought feta, mozzarella, or cottage cheese and 80 percent less than store-bought Romano and Parmesan!

4 Its fresh taste is unbeatable.

5 You need no special equipment! No thermometer, no rennet purchased on the Internet, no acetic acid crystals, no citric acid crystals; even the cheesecloth is optional. If you have ever tried cheese making before, you know that you have been required to buy all of these. No more!

6 It's self-reliant and completely local since it uses kefir grains, a yeast and bacteria starter.

7 You get to control the amount of salt in the cheese.

8 It's fun. And it's the only cheese recipe in the world that begins with a shovel!

WHY CHEESE MAKING?

y fascination with homemade cheese making was jump-started like a firestorm in February 2014 when I stumbled upon this headline: "World's Oldest Cheese Found on Mummies."

Global news outlets told the story: protein chunks found on necklaces worn by newly discovered Chinese mummies were, in fact, kefir cheese. The *Journal of Archaeological Science* announced the findings of chemists at Germany's Max Planck Institute of Molecular Cell Biology and Genetics. And it was not just any cheese—it was the world's oldest confirmed cheese, by a long shot. The mummies had been essentially vacuum-packed in tight leather casings and buried in a desert where dry soil and salt preserved them nearly perfectly.

None of this, however, was what caught my eye. What fascinated me were the words "kefir" and "necklace." Using kefir grains is an ancient way of making a yogurt-like food from milk. Kefir grains are a combination of beneficial bacteria and yeast that naturally removes the lactose from milk and turns it into yogurt at room temperature. I knew that kefir grains had been used worldwide for thousands of years. I had kefir milk in my fridge. I drank kefir for its health benefits (it is a natural probiotic). I had known that people made some soft cheeses from kefir, too. But I had never heard of anyone making hard cheese from kefir.

Having some experience with soft cheese, I also knew it would be nearly impossible to make beads of soft cheese to put on a necklace. There was no way that the 3,600-year-old cheese in China was soft. But chemists had confirmed beyond a doubt that it was kefir cheese. Hard kefir cheese.

Here was proof beyond a doubt that hard cheese, made of kefir, had once existed. I was immediately determined to re-create this ancient recipe.

WHY BACKYARD RENNET?

ennet is the word that cheese makers use to describe a variety of naturally occurring enzymes that are capable of producing hard cheese when used correctly. Almost all rennet available today is synthetic—created in laboratories. If you want to make cheese, there is a line of companies ready to sell you rennet. The problem is that rennet does not self-produce, so you have to buy it every time you want to make cheese. This violates what I think of as the natural law of abundance—prosperity always arrives in abundance, with enough for everyone. (I could write a book on this subject. Perhaps one day . . .) For example, kefir is self-producing; once you have kefir grains, you have them for life, you don't have to buy them again, and you can give them away to anyone who wants them, because they multiply. The same is true of natural baking yeast, all animals that people eat for food, and all heirloom vegetables that people eat for food (before the invention of hybrids and patents and lawyers, which all violate the law of abundance).

My point is this: it was clear and obvious to me that 3,600 years ago, there had to be an easy, abundant way to get rennet. Rennet, as it occurs in nature, comes in both animal and vegetable varieties. So I started looking for a source of backyard vegetable rennet. I didn't have to look far.

///

MALVA NEGLECTA

For a long time, I've been fascinated with the uses of the plant that scientists call *Malva neglecta*—the rest of us call it "mallow," "common mallow," or "dwarf mallow," and most people know it as "cheeseplant" or "cheeseweed." Mallow is one of the world's most amazing plants. The root can be used to make powerful medicine for sinus infections, colds, flu, coughs, and asthma. (We practice herbal medicine at our house.) I use it to make hand soap and dishwashing soap, as has been done for hundreds of years. I use the plant to make homemade marshmallows, something also done for hundreds of years.

We eat the leaves in salad and consume the peas. It is such an important plant, which is why the settlers of the country brought it to America in the first place.

So why is it called "cheeseplant" or "cheeseweed"?

You don't have to go far on the Internet to find "the answer." Thousands of sites will tell you it is because mallow peas look like tiny rounds of cheese. For years, I have thought this answer was nonsense. Historically, people have named plants after important uses. For example, soapwort is a flower that I grow in my backyard that has been used for thousands of years to make soap. We know it was used in the time of Christ to make soap (you can look for my soapwort guidebook as part of the *Backyard Renaissance* series). Few people know anything about soapwort today, much less use it, but if you are paying attention, you can still find original pioneer patches of soapwort flowers, which they regularly used to make simple homemade soap. This is just one example of how plants have historically been named after their uses.

EXPERIMENTATION

For a long time, I had suspected that mallow was used as rennet to make cheese. It wasn't until I read about the world's oldest cheese that I began to wonder if kefir plus mallow would equal hard cheese. So I started to experiment.

I made cheese almost every day from February until June. Sometimes I made three batches of cheese in a day. I was determined to figure out how to make self-sufficient cheese. It wasn't easy, but through lots of trial and error, I found some answers.

Making cheese requires only two things—milk and acid. The reason that kefir is used to make cheese, I discovered, is simple. Kefir greatly lowers the pH of milk. Kefir is between 3 and 4 on the pH scale, making it a pretty good acid. Most current cheese recipes call for the use of lemon juice as an acid. Lemons are common today, but in most places, cheese could not have been made using lemon juice 3,600 years ago. But kefir, we know for a fact, *was* in use 3,600 years ago.

Through my experiments, I discovered that kefir alone provides enough acid to trigger the production of curd in milk.

But milk plus acid makes only soft cheese. To make hard cheese, you have to use rennet. I suspected cheeseplant (mallow) was a natural source of rennet. So I started cooking.

And I got nothing. It was a failure.

I began searching the Internet. I searched deep and wide. I searched scientific journals and cheese making books—and I found a handful of references to people who had "heard" that mallow could be used to make cheese. But after many hours of research, I was not able to find anyone who had actually used mallow to make cheese—no one with experience. So there was no one who could tell me why my mallow cheese experiments were going nowhere.

Then, one day in the kitchen, it dawned on me that I was doing it all wrong. I knew rennet was a naturally occurring enzyme on mallow, and I had assumed that the enzyme existed on the leaves of the plant. But what if it was in the root? I went into my backyard and dug up a mallow root.

And I made excellent cheese.

I was thrilled that I had cracked the code, but doubly thrilled to find an extra bonus—not only did the root produce hard cheese, but *it nearly doubled the amount of curd that I got from the same volume of milk.*

Why does this matter? Because suddenly, the cheese I was making was cheaper, ounce for ounce, than the cheese for sale in the grocery store. (And making Romano or Parmesan cheese is drastically cheaper.) To me, it was a huge self-reliance breakthrough.

Since my discovery, I have tried literally every variation of this recipe I could imagine. I have tried different amounts of root to produce rennet, I have tried different temperatures, I have tried different timing, and I have tried making different kinds of cheeses. After months of work, I am excited to say that I have perfected this recipe. I have re-created what I believe to be the only recipe in existence that makes it possible to make hard cheese in any climate.

KEfiR

This recipe requires culturing kefir, which is an ancient process of making a yogurt-like probiotic from milk. Kefir is produced at home by adding kefir grains to milk at room temperature. Kefir grains are a white, gelatin-like "blob" (for lack of a better word) of beneficial yeast and bacteria that convert milk into a thick, yogurt-like substance. To this day, kefir is still used by nomadic Bedouin tribes on the African continent, made with goat milk in goat skin containers. Kefir is very simple to make.

Kefir is used widely across the United States for its health benefits. Because kefir slowly multiplies, people are usually happy to give kefir grains to anyone who asks for them. You should not have to pay for kefir grains. If you are new to kefir, here is a list of suggestions to get started:

- Ask about kefir users or classes at local health food stores and in online communities. Wherever you live, there are likely many people nearby who are using kefir.
- Ask for kefir on social media. Use your Facebook, or join a Facebook group dedicated to probiotics, kefir, cultured

food, or health food. Ask on Twitter or any other social media site.

- Search on websites. Ask for kefir grains on Craigslist.org, on Freecycle.org, or on your community's favorite "give stuff away for free" website. In the county where I live, there are more than a dozen Facebook pages dedicated to people who want to give things away for free, including kefir grains and starts of natural baking yeast.

- Join my email list. When I have kefir grains available, I will offer them on my email newsletter list. (I don't charge for kefir grains, but you will need to pay for shipping.) You can join by going to http://calebwarnock.com/sp/email/ or by going to CalebWarnock.blogspot.com and clicking on "Join Caleb's Email List."

MAKING KEFIR

SUPPLIES

- Glass quart jar
- Sieve, slotted spoon, or colander

INGREDIENTS

- 1 quart milk
- 1–2 teaspoons kefir grains

DIRECTIONS

STEP 1: Put the kefir grains into a glass quart jar or another non-metallic container and fill it nearly full with whole milk. You can put your kefir in any amount of milk, but keep in mind that the less milk the kefir is in, the faster the milk will turn into kefir. For the purposes of this cheese recipe, you will need roughly 1 quart of milk. Any amount from 3/4 quart to 1 full quart will work.

STEP 2: Cover the container with a lid and put it someplace in the kitchen that is room temperature and away from direct sunlight. **Do not** refrigerate at this time. **Do not** stir or agitate. Kefir is most often used as a drink, and you do not want your kefir to be sour when drinking it. Kefir made for drinking is usually left at room temperature for 6–12 hours; much longer, and the kefir will be sour. However, for making cheese, you *must* have sour (acidic) kefir. Don't worry; the sourness will be completely gone from the final cheese product.

STEP 3: Your kefir is ready for cheese making after 24 hours at room temperature (up to 48 hours maximum). After 24–48 hours, you should put the entire container of kefir into the fridge if you are not going to use it immediately; the cold will stop the curdling action. At this point, your kefir should be very thick and have a clear water-like liquid at the bottom of the container. The kefir at the very top of the jar may yellow or darken because it is exposed to oxygen inside the container; this is normal. Kefir, with its grains, can be left in the fridge for 1–2 weeks if necessary.

STEP 4: To continue preparing your kefir, you should pour the kefir through a sieve, slotted spoon, or colander to capture the kefir grains. All the grains will be at the top of the container. Put the grains back into the empty container and fill it with another quart of milk, and start the process over. Kefir grains double in size about every twenty days if they are being fed regularly (every couple days). If they spend most of their time in the fridge, they double much more slowly. After your kefir grains have doubled, you can give half the grains away or compost them, feed them to chickens or dogs, or throw them away (if you must). You can also freeze or dry them for later use.

CHEESE-MAKING RECIPES

TIPS FOR CHEESE-MAKING SUCCESS

- Don't stir the milk. Curd is extremely fragile until it is fully formed. It does not like to be touched or moved at all. Stirring can destroy your cheese.

- You can use either pasteurized whole milk from the grocery store or raw milk. Raw milk makes more curd and a more flavorful cheese. Raw milk is pasteurized in the process of this recipe, so you don't have to worry about bad bacteria. Store-bought whole milk also works great in this recipe.

- Don't use skim, 1-percent, or 2-percent milk. Milk fat is a necessary ingredient in cheese making, so you will get much less cheese for your time and effort if you use anything but whole-fat milk.

- Don't waste the whey! When you finish this recipe, you will have about half of a gallon of whey left over. You can use this whey to replace half a gallon of the primary liquid ingredient in Caleb Warnock's Guaranteed Edible Weedkiller Recipe (available at SeedRenaissance.com). You can feed the whey to your dog or cat, put it in your compost pile, use it to boil pasta (delicious!), or use it in many other ways.

- If you do use raw milk, you will find that curd also forms on the bottom of the pan, so you will want to gently scrape the bottom of the pan with a spatula or spoon to capture that curd. Pasteurized milk does not form significant curd on the bottom of the pan.

- Mallow grows all over the United States as a weed. You should be able to find mallow root growing wild wherever you live. If you cannot find it immediately, contact your local university extension service or local herbalists for help. There is an offer for free mallow seed in this guidebook.

SEVEN KEFIR CHEESES MADE WITH BACKYARD RENNET

This is an ascending recipe, meaning that the further you follow the recipe, the more varieties of cheese you will be able to make. You will begin the recipe and stop after Step 4 to make cottage cheese, continue to Step 6 to make feta cheese, continue to Step 8 to make cream cheese, continue to Step 9 Option A to make mozzarella cheese, or continue Step 9 Option B to make white cheddar cheese. Complete Step 10 for Romano cheese or Step 11 for Parmesan cheese.

At this writing, my homemade cheese costs 19 cents per ounce ($3.04 per pound), about 25 percent less than grocery store yellow cheese and 40 percent less than mozzarella or white cheddar from the grocery store. Making homemade Romano and Parmesan costs about *80 percent less* than buying cheese at the grocery store.

SUPPLIES

- 4-quart stainless steel pan
- Sieve or colander

- Slotted spoon
- Spatula
- Cheesecloth or voile straining fabric
- Wooden spoon
- Microwave-safe stoneware or glass bowl

INGREDIENTS

- 1/2 gallon + 2 cups whole or raw milk
- 1 quart kefir (minus the grains)
- 1 washed fresh mallow root
- Salt (optional)

DIRECTIONS

STEP 1: Add 1/2 gallon of the milk to a large stainless steel 4-quart pan (or larger) with a thick bottom. The pan must have a thick bottom or the cheese will scald. On medium-low heat, slowly heat the milk until it is warm enough that you can feel the warmth but not so hot that it is uncomfortable if you taste it or put your finger into it.

STEP 2: When the milk is warm, remove the grains from your kefir. Pour the kefir into the milk. Do not stir.

STEP 3: Put 2 cups of milk into a blender. Chop the mallow root into 1-inch sections and blend it into the milk for 20 seconds. Pour the mallow-root milk through a sieve into the pan of milk on the stove. In the sieve, you will find mallow root strings; you can throw these away. You may stir *once* across the pan at this point to mix this into the pot.

STEP 4: Wait and observe as the cheese begins to form curd in the pan. When the curd is obviously lumpy, it can be removed with a slotted spoon to be used as cottage cheese. If you want cottage cheese, you are now done with this recipe. If you want other cheeses, continue on.

STEP 5: Let the mixture cook for another 20 minutes. This will allow the cheese to "break," that is, all the milk fat will turn to curd and only pale yellow whey will remain. There will be no more milk in the pan. There are two ways to check if the cheese has broken without stirring. First, you will see the pan of milk begin to form spouts of boiling bubbles in places. Second, you can take a spatula or knife and carefully pull the curd back from the edge of the pan just enough to see that whey has formed. Whey is a pale yellow, semi-clear liquid. It does not resemble milk at all. If you still see milk, your curd is not done forming and you should wait 2–3 more minutes then check for whey again.

STEP 6: Using a slotted spoon, strain the curd into a colander or sieve with a bowl beneath it to catch the dripping whey. When the whey has stopped dripping, the remaining curd can be used as feta cheese. If you want other cheeses instead of feta, continue on.

STEP 7: To encourage the whey to drain, press the curd in the colander with the back of a spoon or spatula. You should now salt the cheese to taste if you wish. You don't have to salt the cheese if you don't want to, but everyone who has taken cheese-making classes from me has preferred salted cheese. I usually make unsalted cheese so that I can add salt to my cheese dishes later when I am making home-made macaroni and cheese, for example.

STEP 8: To make cream cheese, when the whey has stopped dripping, put the curd into cheese-cloth* or voile fabric and tie it onto the center of a wooden spoon handle. Standing over the sink, twist the spoon repeatedly to remove as much whey as possible. Let the curd cure in the fridge for about 12 hours. You may now use this as cream cheese.

*NOTE: CHEESECLOTH IS DIFFICULT TO CLEAN AND RE-USE. VOILE FABRIC IS EASY TO CLEAN AND CAN BE REUSED FOR MAKING CHEESE OR HERBAL REMEDIES OVER AND OVER AGAIN. VOILE STRAINING FABRIC IS AVAILABLE AT SEEDRENAISSANCE.COM.

STEP 9, OPTION A: To make mozzarella cheese, put the curd into a microwave-safe stoneware or glass bowl. Heat for 60 seconds on high. Remove from microwave and immediately drain any whey. Knead the cheese with a spatula by folding the cheese onto itself for 1–2 minutes. Microwave again for 30 seconds and knead. Microwave again for 30 seconds and knead. When the cheese becomes shiny, form it into a ball and put it into a bowl of heavily salted ice water for at least an hour or overnight. Cut and serve. You can store this cheese for several days in the bowl of iced salt water if you desire.

STEP 9, OPTION B: To make white cheddar cheese instead of mozzarella cheese, remove the curd from the colander (see Step 8), put it into cheesecloth or voile fabric, and tie the fabric into a loose bundle. Place the bundle into a cheese press if you have one available. If you don't have a cheese press, you can use clean, boiled stones or other weights and press your cheesecloth bundle in a sieve in the fridge (with a bowl underneath to catch the dripping whey*). Add a few more ounces every couple of hours.

*NOTE: IF YOU DO NOT REMOVE ENOUGH WHEY, THE CHEESE WILL NEVER BECOME CHEDDAR; IT WILL RE-MAIN AS CREAM CHEESE AND WILL NOT BE GRATE-ABLE.

When you are done pressing the cheese, it will need to be refrigerated overnight to set up. *Do not cover the cheese in the refrigerator*. Do not put it into plastic or any kind of lidded container. Just put the whole bundle into the refriegerator in an open bowl or on a plate. The next day, you can carefully remove the wrapping and grate the cheese.* If you are using voile fabric, you can soak the fabric in hot water and rub it together to clean it for reuse.

*NOTE: THIS WILL BE MILD CHEDDAR. IF YOU WANT ME-DIUM CHEDDAR, AFTER THE FIRST DAY, PUT THE CHEESE IN A CONTAINER WITH A LID AND LET IT AGE IN THE FRIDGE UNTIL YOU LIKE THE TASTE (ABOUT 3 DAYS). IF YOU WANT SHARP CHEDDAR, LET IT AGE LONGER IN THE FRIDGE (ABOUT 6 DAYS).

STEP 10: To make a Romano-style dry cheese, after pressing your cheese, let it sit in the fridge for a week in its cheesecloth or voile fabric. The cheese *must not* be in a covered container. Set the cheese on a plate, tied inside the cloth, and do not cover it. This allows the cheese to begin to dry out. After about a week, you will have a Romano-type cheese.

STEP 11: To make a Parmesan-style cheese, leave the uncovered cheese, still in the fabric, in the fridge for 2 weeks or longer. The cheese will begin to smell like Parmesan—and it will be delicious on pasta.

QUESTIONS AND ANSWERS

You may have further questions about cheese making. Here are a few I've received.

QUESTION: You said raw milk is pasteurized in the process of making this cheese. Can you explain?

ANSWER: Pasteurization is the process of heating milk to kill bad bacteria. I am not against raw milk—in fact, I grew up on raw milk. I milked our family cow. My grandpa Robert Warnock milked cows. My mother and grandmother both made homemade butter, and we had milk and cream coming out of our ears. My father once bartered our raw milk in exchange for handmade beds for my sister and me. We were meticulous in making sure our milk was clean, but "meticulous" is less and less possible today because instead of family farms, our milk tends to be supplied by people who are paid minimum wage and are not taking the milk home with them for their own families to drink. So be wise and careful. People die from raw milk—but a lot more people die from driving cars.

Oregon State University Extension Service says this about the definition of pasteurization: "Raw milk can be a source of dangerous microorganisms that pose serious health risks. Several foodborne illness outbreaks in the Pacific Northwest and elsewhere in the United States have been traced to drinking raw milk. Home pasteurization is a good safeguard against possible risk of illness. The heat of pasteurization kills harmful bacteria such as Salmonella, Listeria, and E. coli O157:H7. These disease-causing bacteria can even be in raw milk that is produced with good sanitation practices. It's especially important to pasteurize raw milk that will be consumed by people who are susceptible to foodborne illness. That includes pregnant women, young children, older adults, and those with cancer, HIV/AIDS, and other immune system diseases. For best quality, raw milk must be heated slowly during pasteurization. . . . Use a meat or candy thermometer to determine when the temperature reaches 165 degrees F and keep it at this temperature for 15 seconds."[1]

Because my cheese recipe exceeds 165 degrees for 15 seconds, the raw milk is pasteurized in the process of making cheese (if you are using raw milk). You can use a cooking thermometer to test this for yourself.

QUESTION: Is mallow root safe to use?

ANSWER: Yes! Mallow root has been used for thousands of years for many purposes, not the least of which is to make marshmallows. The marshmallows you buy in the grocery store don't contain real mallow anymore, but for centuries, mallow root was the only way to make marshmallows. I still make them from mallow root, carrying on the old tradition. I will also point out that you are not eating any root in this recipe—you are simply blending the root with milk to capture the enzymes and then sieving out the root. We know for a fact that rennet enzymes are safe; they have been used for thousands of years and are still used in all hard cheese made in the world today. However, mallow root is *not* safe to use if you are not sure of what you are harvesting. Never use any root or herb unless you *know* you are harvesting the correct plant. Not sure? Consult an herbalist or horticulturalist in your area, or call your local university extension service.

QUESTION: Are there other sources of natural vegetable rennet?

ANSWER: Good question! I have heard that stinging nettle is a source of natural rennet. I use nettle all the time to control my allergies (I make nettle tea or a nettle infusion), but I have not yet tried to make cheese with it, simply because fresh nettle is much harder to come by than mallow. I would have to experiment to find out if it really works, whether it works the same, whether to use the root or the leaves, etc. And you obviously have to be very careful harvesting stinging nettle.

QUESTION: How much weight do you suggest we put on the cheddar cheese?

ANSWER: The weight I start with is 1 pound 3 ounces. Then I add another pound, and I end up with about 3 pounds overnight to make cheddar.

QUESTION: I am assuming the mallow root should be 1 1/2 inches long and also assuming it really doesn't matter how thick it is. Is that correct?

ANSWER: The root needs to be at least an ounce, which is 1 1/2 inches if the root is about 1/2 inch in diameter.

FREE OFFER: TO GET FREE MALVA NEGLECTA SEED, GO TO CALEBWARNOCK.BLOGSPOT.COM AND CLICK ON "FREE OFFERS."

SOURCES

1. http://extension.oregonstate.edu/lane/sites/default/files/
documents/sp_50-932home_pasteurizationofrawmilk_.pdf

ABOUT THE AUTHOR

Caleb Warnock is the popular author of *Forgotten Skills of Self-Sufficiency Used by the Mormon Pioneers*, *The Art of Baking with Natural Yeast*, *Backyard Winter Gardening For All Climates*, *More Forgotten Skills*, *Trouble's On The Menu*, and more. He is the owner of SeedRenaissance.com and blogs at CalebWarnock.blogspot.com, where you will find a link to join his email list to learn more about forgotten skills.

ABOUT FAMILIUS

VISIT OUR WEBSITE: www.familius.com

JOIN OUR FAMILY: There are lots of ways to connect with us! Subscribe to our newsletters at www.familius.com to receive uplifting daily inspiration, essays from our Pater Familius, a free ebook every month, and the first word on special discounts and Familius news.

GET BULK DISCOUNTS: If you feel a few friends and family might benefit from what you've read, let us know and we'll be happy to provide you with quantity discounts. Simply email us at specialorders@familius.com.

CONNECT:
www.facebook.com/paterfamilius
@familiustalk, @paterfamilius1
www.pinterest.com/familius

FAMILIUS

THE MOST IMPORTANT WORK YOU EVER DO WILL BE WITHIN THE WALLS OF YOUR OWN HOME.

Lightning Source UK Ltd.
Milton Keynes UK
UKOW02f0758280716

279425UK00003B/18/P